RESPIRATORY TOXICOLOGY

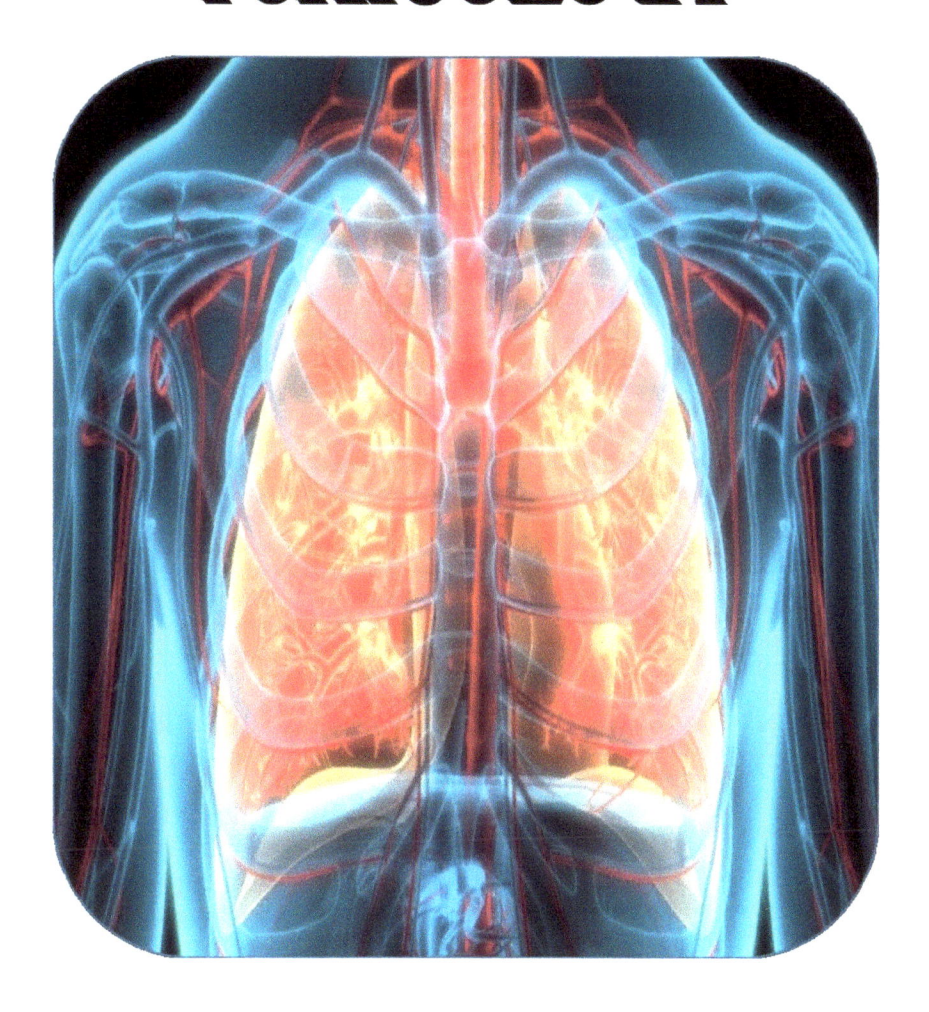

TABLE OF CONTENTS

INTRODUCTION 2

MODULE ONE 3

    LESSON ONE: RESPIRATORY TOXICOLOGY 3

    LESSON TWO: FUNDAMENTAL CONCEPTS IN RESPIRATORY TOXICOLOGY 7

MODULE TWO 11

    LESSON ONE: COMMON RESPIRATORY TOXINS AND THEIR MECHANISMS 11

    LESSON TWO: CLINICAL PRESENTATION AND DIAGNOSIS OF RESPIRATORY TOXICITY 15

MODULE THREE 19

    LESSON ONE: MANAGEMENT AND TREATMENT OF RESPIRATORY TOXICITY 19

    LESSON TWO: PREVENTIVE STRATEGIES IN RESPIRATORY TOXICOLOGY 22

MODULE FOUR 26

    LESSON ONE: CASE STUDIES IN RESPIRATORY TOXICOLOGY 26

MODULE FIVE 30

    LESSON ONE: FUTURE DIRECTIONS IN RESPIRATORY TOXICOLOGY 30

MODULE SIX 33

    LESSON ONE: ETHICAL AND LEGAL CONSIDERATIONS IN RESPIRATORY TOXICOLOGY 33

MODULE SEVEN 37
   LESSON ONE: INTEGRATIVE AND HOLISTIC
   APPROACHES TO RESPIRATORY HEALTH 37

CONCLUSION 41

REFERENCES 42

COURSE OVERVIEW

This course provides a comprehensive exploration of respiratory toxicology, focusing on the mechanisms, clinical manifestations, diagnosis, management, and preventive strategies related to respiratory exposures in occupational and environmental settings. Participants will gain insights into the complexities of respiratory toxicity, from basic principles to advanced diagnostic and treatment modalities. The course emphasizes a multidisciplinary approach, integrating knowledge from toxicology, epidemiology, clinical medicine, and public health to enhance understanding and promote effective management of respiratory health hazards.

COURSE OBJECTIVES

By the end of this course, participants will be able to understand Fundamental Concepts in Respiratory Toxicology, Common Respiratory Toxins and Their Mechanisms, Clinical Presentation and Diagnosis of Respiratory Toxicity, Management and Treatment of Respiratory Toxicity, Preventive Strategies in Respiratory Toxicology, Case Studies in Respiratory Toxicology, and Future Directions in Respiratory Toxicology

COURSE MATERIAL

To learn this course, **healthcare providers/ participants** must be provided with materials like a Pen, pencil, notebook, and notepad to better understand and make it easy for them to learn.

INTRODUCTION

In today's fast-paced and industrialized world, respiratory toxicology has emerged as a critical field of study for healthcare providers. The respiratory system, being the primary interface between the external environment and the body's internal milieu, is particularly vulnerable to various toxins. From air pollution and occupational exposures to chemical warfare agents and household chemicals, the sources of respiratory toxins are diverse and omnipresent. Therefore, a deep understanding of respiratory toxicology is essential for healthcare providers to effectively diagnose, manage, and prevent respiratory toxicities in their patients.

"Mastering Respiratory Toxicology: A Comprehensive Course for Healthcare Providers" is designed to be an informative and engaging resource that equips healthcare professionals with the knowledge and skills necessary to navigate the complexities of this field. This book aims to bridge the gap between basic toxicological principles and clinical practice, providing a holistic approach to respiratory toxicology.

MODULE ONE

LESSON ONE: RESPIRATORY TOXICOLOGY

Respiratory toxicology is a specialized field within toxicology that focuses on the effects of toxic substances on the respiratory system. The respiratory system, which includes the nose, throat, trachea, bronchi, and lungs, is highly susceptible to toxicants due to its constant exposure to the external environment. The primary function of the respiratory system is gas exchange, a vital process that supports cellular respiration and overall metabolic function. Any impairment in this system can have profound effects on health, making the study of respiratory toxicology critically important.

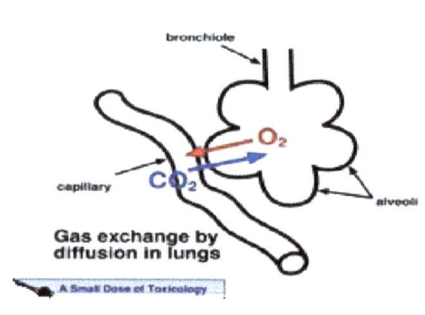

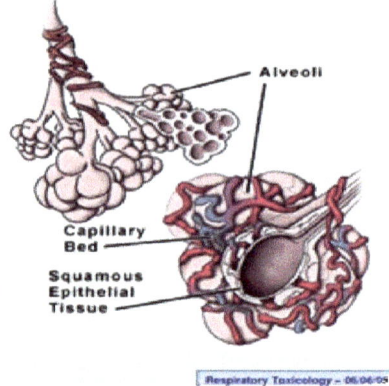

Historical Evolution

The recognition of respiratory toxicology as a distinct field has evolved over centuries. Ancient civilizations were aware of the harmful effects of certain substances on the respiratory system. For instance, miners in ancient Greece and Rome experienced respiratory problems due to inhalation of dust and fumes. However, it was not until the Industrial Revolution in the 18th and 19th centuries that respiratory toxicology began to gain prominence. The rapid industrialization led to increased exposure to a wide range of pollutants, prompting scientific inquiry into their health effects.

The early 20th century saw significant advancements in the understanding of respiratory toxicology. Landmark studies, such as those on coal workers' pneumoconiosis (black lung disease) and asbestos-related diseases, highlighted the occupational hazards faced by workers and the need for regulatory measures to protect respiratory health. These studies laid the groundwork for modern respiratory toxicology by establishing links between specific toxicants and respiratory diseases.

Importance of Respiratory Toxicology

Respiratory toxicology is crucial for several reasons. First and foremost, respiratory diseases are a leading cause of morbidity and mortality worldwide. Conditions such as asthma, chronic obstructive pulmonary disease (COPD), and lung cancer are often associated with exposure to respiratory toxins. Understanding the mechanisms by which these toxins cause harm is essential for developing effective prevention and treatment strategies.

Secondly, the respiratory system serves as a primary route of entry for many toxicants. Inhalation is a common exposure pathway for airborne pollutants, chemicals, and biological agents. Once inhaled, these substances can exert local effects on the respiratory tract or be absorbed into the bloodstream, leading to systemic toxicity. Therefore, respiratory toxicology encompasses both local and systemic effects of inhaled toxicants.

Scope of Respiratory Toxicology

The scope of respiratory toxicology is broad, encompassing various aspects of toxicant exposure, mechanism of action, and health effects. It includes the study of:

- Air Pollutants: Common air pollutants such as particulate matter (PM), nitrogen oxides (NOx), sulfur dioxide (SO_2), carbon monoxide (CO), and ozone (O_3) are well-known respiratory toxicants. These pollutants can cause a range of

respiratory problems, from mild irritation to severe lung diseases.
- Occupational Exposures: Workers in certain industries are at increased risk of exposure to respiratory toxicants. For example, miners, construction workers, and chemical industry workers may be exposed to dust, asbestos, silica, and various industrial chemicals that can harm the respiratory system.
- Chemical Warfare Agents: Certain chemicals, such as mustard gas and chlorine gas, have been used as weapons of war due to their severe respiratory effects. Understanding the toxicology of these agents is important for medical and military personnel.
- Household Chemicals: Everyday household products, including cleaning agents, paints, and pesticides, can release volatile organic compounds (VOCs) that may cause respiratory irritation or other health issues.
- Biological Agents: Pathogens such as bacteria, viruses, and fungi can produce toxins that affect the respiratory system. Additionally, biological allergens like mold spores and pollen can trigger respiratory conditions like asthma and allergic rhinitis.

Interdisciplinary Nature

Respiratory toxicology is inherently interdisciplinary, intersecting with fields such as pulmonology, occupational medicine, environmental health, and pharmacology. Healthcare providers, including physicians, nurses, respiratory therapists, and public health professionals, need to collaborate to address the complex challenges posed by respiratory toxicants. This interdisciplinary approach ensures comprehensive care for patients and effective strategies for preventing respiratory toxicities.

Respiratory toxicology is a vital field that addresses the impact of toxic substances on the respiratory system. Its historical evolution underscores the importance of recognizing and mitigating respiratory hazards. As healthcare providers, understanding the principles and applications of respiratory toxicology is essential for improving patient outcomes and promoting public health.

DISCUSSION QUESTIONS

- What are the primary sources of respiratory toxins in occupational and environmental settings, and how do they affect respiratory health?
- Discuss the importance of studying respiratory toxicology in the context of public health and occupational safety

LESSON TWO: FUNDAMENTAL CONCEPTS IN RESPIRATORY TOXICOLOGY

Understanding the fundamental concepts of respiratory toxicology is crucial for healthcare providers to effectively diagnose, manage, and prevent respiratory toxicities. This lesson will cover the anatomy and physiology of the respiratory system, the principles of toxicokinetics and toxicodynamics, and the factors influencing respiratory toxicity.

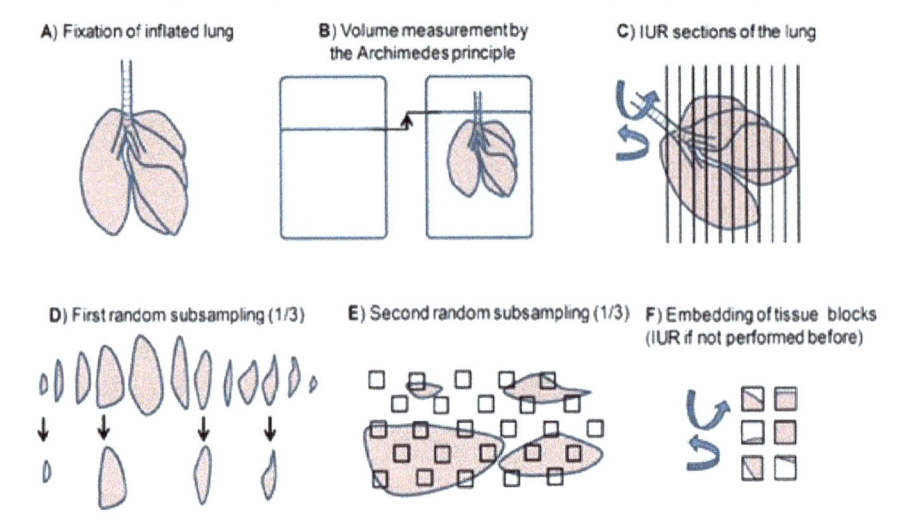

A) Fixation of inflated lung

B) Volume measurement by the Archimedes principle

C) IUR sections of the lung

D) First random subsampling (1/3)

E) Second random subsampling (1/3)

F) Embedding of tissue blocks (IUR if not performed before)

Anatomy and Physiology of the Respiratory System

The respiratory system is responsible for the exchange of gases between the external environment and the bloodstream. It is divided into the upper and lower respiratory tracts:

- Upper Respiratory Tract: Includes the nose, nasal cavity, sinuses, pharynx, and larynx. These structures filter, warm, and humidify incoming air, preparing it for entry into the lower respiratory tract.
- Lower Respiratory Tract: Comprises the trachea, bronchi, bronchioles, and alveoli. The trachea bifurcates into the right and left bronchi, which further divide into smaller

bronchioles, culminating in the alveoli where gas exchange occurs.

Principles of Toxicokinetics

- Toxicokinetics refers to the processes of absorption, distribution, metabolism, and excretion (ADME) of toxicants. Understanding these principles helps in predicting the behavior of inhaled toxicants within the body:
- Absorption: Inhaled toxicants are absorbed through the respiratory mucosa into the bloodstream. The alveolar surface area and the thin barrier between alveoli and capillaries facilitate rapid absorption.
- Distribution: Once absorbed, toxicants are distributed throughout the body via the circulatory system. Lipid-soluble toxicants can easily cross cell membranes and accumulate in fatty tissues, while water-soluble toxicants remain in the extracellular fluid.
- Metabolism: The liver is the primary site for the metabolism of toxicants, where they are converted into more water-soluble compounds for easier excretion. However, the respiratory system also contains metabolic enzymes that can activate or detoxify inhaled substances.
- Excretion: Toxicants and their metabolites are excreted primarily through the kidneys (urine) and the liver (bile). The respiratory system can also excrete volatile substances through exhalation.

Principles of Toxicodynamics

Toxicodynamics involves the interaction of toxicants with biological targets and the subsequent effects on the body. Key concepts include:

- Mechanism of Action: Toxicants can cause harm through various mechanisms, such as oxidative stress, inflammation, cellular damage, and interference with cellular signaling pathways.

- Dose-Response Relationship: The severity of toxic effects is often related to the dose and duration of exposure. Understanding the dose-response relationship helps in assessing risk and establishing safety thresholds.
- Target Organs: Inhaled toxicants primarily affect the respiratory system, but they can also have systemic effects on other organs. Identifying the target organs helps in predicting and managing toxicities.

Factors Influencing Respiratory Toxicity

Several factors influence the severity and outcome of respiratory toxicity:

- Chemical Properties: The physical and chemical properties of a toxicant, such as solubility, reactivity, and particle size, determine its behavior in the respiratory system and its potential to cause harm.
- Exposure Conditions: The concentration, duration, and frequency of exposure are critical determinants of toxicity. Acute high-level exposures can cause immediate effects, while chronic low-level exposures can lead to cumulative damage.
- Individual Susceptibility: Genetic factors, age, sex, pre-existing health conditions, and lifestyle choices (e.g., smoking) can influence an individual's susceptibility to respiratory toxicants.
- Environmental Factors: Ambient air quality, workplace conditions, and indoor air pollution contribute to overall exposure levels and can modulate the risk of respiratory toxicity.

Understanding the fundamental concepts of respiratory toxicology provides a solid foundation for healthcare providers to navigate the complexities of this field. By comprehending the anatomy and physiology of the respiratory system, the principles of toxicokinetics and toxicodynamics, and the factors influencing respiratory toxicity, healthcare providers can better predict, diagnose, and manage respiratory toxicities.

DISCUSSION QUESTIONS

- What are the primary mechanisms by which respiratory toxins cause damage to the lungs at a cellular and molecular level?
- Discuss the differences in pathophysiological responses between direct-acting toxins (e.g., gases, particulates) and indirect-acting toxins (e.g., allergens, irritants).

MODULE TWO

LESSON ONE: COMMON RESPIRATORY TOXINS AND THEIR MECHANISMS

In this lesson, we will delve into the various respiratory toxins that healthcare providers may encounter in their practice. Understanding the sources, mechanisms of action, and health effects of these toxins is crucial for effective diagnosis and management.

Summary of Common Chemical Toxins Related to Inhalation Injuries

	Cyanide (CN)	Carbon Monoxide (CO)
Odour	Bitter almonds, some cannot detect	Odourless
Sources	Fires, chemical or synthetic combustion, pesticides and synthetic manufacturing, metal extraction, chemical labs	Combustion of carbon compounds (e.g. engines, cooking stoves in enclosed spaces)
Mechanism	Inhibits mitochondrial cytochrome oxidase - halting aerobic metabolism	High affinity for Hgb, displaces oxygen - decreased oxygen delivery
Signs / Symptoms	**Early or mild effects**: vague - dizziness, headache, nausea, anxiety **Late or severe effects**: tachycardia, hypotension, respiratory depression, seizure, coma; ARDS and pulmonary edema; acidosis	**Vague symptoms** (high index of suspicion required) - confusion, stupor, coma, seizures, and myocardial infarction
Treatment	Supportive (oxygen, mechanical ventilation) **Hydroxocobalamin** 5 g IV over 15min, can repeat	**100% Oxygen** – shortens half-life to ~30-90 min **Hyperbaric oxygen** – shortens half-life to ~20min
Controversies	No longer recommend Sodium Nitrite / Thiosulfate	Logistic barriers and limited evidence for HBO

INDUSTRIAL CHEMICALS

1. **Asbestos**
   - Source: Commonly found in construction materials, insulation, and automotive parts.
   - Mechanism: Inhalation of asbestos fibers causes direct damage to lung tissues, leading to inflammation and fibrosis. Chronic exposure can result in asbestosis, lung cancer, and mesothelioma.
   - Health Effects: Symptoms include shortness of breath, persistent cough, and chest pain. Long-term exposure increases the risk of malignancies.

2. **Silica**
   - Source: Found in mining, construction, and manufacturing industries.
   - Mechanism: Inhaled silica particles induce lung inflammation and fibrosis by triggering the release of inflammatory cytokines and reactive oxygen species.
   - Health Effects: Chronic exposure can lead to silicosis, characterized by progressive lung fibrosis, cough, and dyspnea.

AIR POLLUTANTS

1. **Particulate Matter (PM)**
   - Source: Emitted from vehicles, industrial processes, and combustion of fossil fuels.
   - Mechanism: Fine particles (PM2.5 and smaller) penetrate deep into the lungs, causing oxidative stress, inflammation, and exacerbation of pre-existing lung conditions.
   - Health Effects: Increased risk of respiratory infections, asthma, COPD, and cardiovascular diseases.

2. **Ozone (O_3)**
   - Source: Formed by the reaction of sunlight with pollutants like volatile organic compounds (VOCs) and nitrogen oxides (NOx).
   - Mechanism: Ozone is a powerful oxidant that damages the respiratory epithelium, leading to inflammation and decreased lung function.
   - Health Effects: Symptoms include chest pain, coughing, throat irritation, and airway inflammation. Chronic exposure can reduce lung function and worsen respiratory diseases.

CHEMICAL WARFARE AGENTS

1. **Mustard Gas**
   - Source: Used in chemical warfare.
   - Mechanism: Alkylates DNA and proteins, causing cell death and severe tissue damage.

- Health Effects: Acute exposure results in severe respiratory tract irritation, blistering, and pulmonary edema. Long-term effects include chronic bronchitis and increased risk of lung cancer.

2. **Chlorine Gas**
   - Source: Used in water treatment, cleaning products, and industrial processes.
   - Mechanism: Reacts with moisture in the respiratory tract to form hydrochloric acid and hypochlorous acid, causing corrosive damage to tissues.
   - Health Effects: Acute exposure leads to coughing, choking, and difficulty breathing. Severe exposure can cause pulmonary edema and acute respiratory distress syndrome (ARDS).

HOUSEHOLD CHEMICALS

1. **Volatile Organic Compounds (VOCs)**
   - Source: Emitted from paints, cleaning agents, solvents, and building materials.
   - Mechanism: VOCs like formaldehyde and benzene are inhaled and can cause irritation of the respiratory tract, as well as systemic toxicity.
   - Health Effects: Short-term exposure results in headaches, dizziness, and respiratory irritation. Long-term exposure is associated with an increased risk of cancer and respiratory diseases.

2. **Carbon Monoxide (CO)**
   - Source: Produced by incomplete combustion of fossil fuels, found in vehicle exhaust, gas appliances, and fires.
   - Mechanism: Binds to hemoglobin with high affinity, reducing the oxygen-carrying capacity of blood and leading to hypoxia.
   - Health Effects: Symptoms include headache, dizziness, confusion, and loss of consciousness. Severe poisoning can be fatal.

BIOLOGICAL AGENTS

1. **Bacterial Toxins**
   - Source: Pathogens like Mycobacterium tuberculosis and Legionella pneumophila.
   - Mechanism: Bacterial toxins can directly damage lung tissues and elicit strong inflammatory responses.
   - Health Effects: Tuberculosis causes chronic cough, hemoptysis, and weight loss. Legionnaires' disease presents with pneumonia-like symptoms, including fever, cough, and chest pain.
2. **Allergens**
   - Source: Pollens, mold spores, animal dander, and dust mites.
   - Mechanism: Allergens trigger immune responses in sensitized individuals, leading to inflammation and bronchoconstriction.
   - Health Effects: Conditions like asthma, allergic rhinitis, and hypersensitivity pneumonitis. Symptoms include wheezing, coughing, nasal congestion, and shortness of breath.

Understanding the common respiratory toxins and their mechanisms of action is vital for healthcare providers. By recognizing the sources and health effects of these toxicants, providers can better diagnose and manage respiratory toxicities.

DISCUSSION QUESTIONS

- What are the primary diagnostic tools used in assessing respiratory toxicity? How do these tools differ in their utility for acute versus chronic toxic exposures?
- Discuss the challenges and limitations associated with diagnosing respiratory toxicity, especially in cases where exposure history may be unclear or multifactorial.

LESSON TWO: CLINICAL PRESENTATION AND DIAGNOSIS OF RESPIRATORY TOXICITY

Accurate diagnosis of respiratory toxicity is essential for timely and effective management. This lesson will guide healthcare providers through the process of recognizing and diagnosing respiratory toxicities, emphasizing the importance of a thorough medical history, physical examination, and appropriate diagnostic tests.

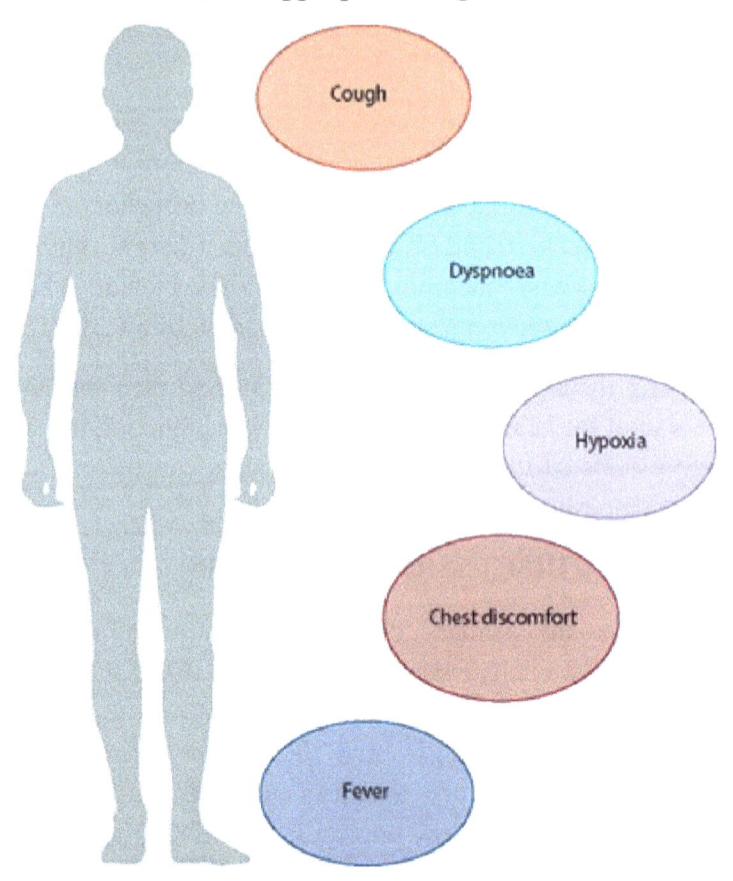

- Cough
- Dyspnoea
- Hypoxia
- Chest discomfort
- Fever

MEDICAL HISTORY

A comprehensive medical history is the first step in diagnosing respiratory toxicity. Key elements include:

1. **Exposure History:**
   - Occupational History: Identify potential exposures at the workplace, such as chemicals, dust, and fumes.
   - Environmental History: Assess exposure to air pollutants, household chemicals, and other environmental toxins.
   - Lifestyle Factors: Inquire about smoking, hobbies, and activities that may involve exposure to respiratory toxins.
2. **Symptom Onset and Duration:**
   - Determine when symptoms began and their progression over time.
   - Establish any correlation between symptom onset and potential exposures.
3. **Medical and Family History:**
   - Document any pre-existing respiratory conditions, such as asthma or COPD.
   - Note any family history of respiratory diseases or sensitivities.

PHYSICAL EXAMINATION

A thorough physical examination can provide valuable clues about respiratory toxicity:

1. **Inspection:**
   - Observe for signs of respiratory distress, such as labored breathing, use of accessory muscles, and cyanosis.
   - Check for physical abnormalities, such as nasal polyps or skin lesions, which may indicate exposure to specific toxins.
2. **Auscultation:**
   - Listen for abnormal breath sounds, such as wheezes, crackles, or diminished breath sounds.
   - Note any changes in lung sounds that may suggest inflammation, fluid accumulation, or airway obstruction.
3. **Palpation and Percussion:**
   - Assess for tenderness, masses, or other abnormalities in the chest wall.
   - Percuss the chest to evaluate for dullness or hyperresonance, which may indicate fluid or air in the pleural space.

DIAGNOSTIC TESTS

Several diagnostic tests can aid in the identification and assessment of respiratory toxicity:

1. **Pulmonary Function Tests (PFTs):**
   - Spirometry: Measures airflow and lung volumes to assess obstructive or restrictive lung disease.
   - Diffusion Capacity: Evaluates the ability of the lungs to transfer gases, useful in detecting interstitial lung diseases.
2. **Imaging Studies:**
   - Chest X-ray: Provides a quick overview of lung and pleural space abnormalities, such as infiltrates, masses, or effusions.
   - High-Resolution Computed Tomography (HRCT): Offers detailed images of lung parenchyma, aiding in the diagnosis of interstitial lung diseases and small airway diseases.
3. **Laboratory Tests:**
   - Blood Gas Analysis: Assesses oxygenation and acid-base status, helping to identify hypoxemia and respiratory acidosis.
   - Biomarkers: Specific biomarkers can indicate exposure to certain toxins. For example, carboxyhemoglobin levels can confirm carbon monoxide poisoning.
4. **Bronchoscopy:**
   - Allows direct visualization of the airways and collection of samples for cytology, microbiology, and histopathology.
   - Useful in diagnosing infections, malignancies, and inflammatory conditions.
5. **Allergy Testing:**
   - Skin prick tests or serum-specific IgE tests can identify sensitivities to common respiratory allergens.

CASE EXAMPLES

1. **Case of Acute Chlorine Gas Exposure:**
   - History: A factory worker presents with acute onset of coughing, chest tightness, and difficulty breathing after a chemical spill.

- Examination: Tachypnea, wheezing, and decreased breath sounds are noted.
- Diagnosis: Chest X-ray shows bilateral infiltrates; blood gas analysis reveals hypoxemia and respiratory acidosis.
- Management: Immediate removal from exposure, administration of oxygen, bronchodilators, and corticosteroids.

2. **Case of Chronic Asbestos Exposure:**
   - History: A retired construction worker with a long history of asbestos exposure presents with progressive dyspnea and dry cough.
   - Examination: Digital clubbing and bilateral basal crackles are observed.
   - Diagnosis: HRCT reveals pleural plaques and interstitial fibrosis; PFTs show restrictive lung disease.
   - Management: Regular monitoring, pulmonary rehabilitation, and supportive care.

Accurate diagnosis of respiratory toxicity requires a systematic approach, incorporating a detailed medical history, thorough physical examination, and appropriate diagnostic tests. By recognizing the clinical presentation and utilizing diagnostic tools effectively, healthcare providers can identify respiratory toxicities early and provide optimal care for their patients.

DISCUSSION QUESTIONS

- What are the common signs and symptoms that suggest respiratory toxicity? How can healthcare providers distinguish between respiratory toxicity and other respiratory conditions, such as asthma exacerbations or infectious pneumonias?
- Discuss the challenges associated with diagnosing respiratory toxicity based on clinical presentation alone, especially in cases with nonspecific symptoms or delayed onset.

MODULE THREE

LESSON ONE: MANAGEMENT AND TREATMENT OF RESPIRATORY TOXICITY

Effective management and treatment of respiratory toxicity involve both acute interventions and long-term strategies to mitigate the effects of toxic exposure. This lesson will cover the various therapeutic approaches, including pharmacological and non-pharmacological interventions, and provide evidence-based guidelines for healthcare providers.

GAS	WATER SOLUBILITY	PRINCIPAL SITE OF RESPIRATORY INJURY
Ammonia	High	Primarily proximal airways, but entire respiratory tract may be affected
Chlorine	Intermediate	Upper and lower respiratory tract
Nitrogen dioxide	Low	Primarily terminal bronchioles and alveoli, but entire respiratory tract may be affected
Phosgene	Low	Alveoli
Sulfur dioxide	High	Proximal and distal airways, including alveoli and bronchioles

ACUTE MANAGEMENT

1. **Removal from Exposure:**
   - The first step in managing acute respiratory toxicity is to immediately remove the patient from the source of exposure.
   - This can involve evacuating the area, providing fresh air, or using personal protective equipment (PPE)

2. **Supportive Care:**
   - Oxygen Therapy: Administer supplemental oxygen to maintain adequate oxygenation, particularly in cases of hypoxemia.
   - Ventilatory Support: In severe cases, mechanical ventilation may be required to support respiratory function.
3. **Pharmacological Interventions:**
   - Bronchodilators: Beta-agonists (e.g., albuterol) and anticholinergics (e.g., ipratropium) can relieve bronchospasm and improve airflow.
   - Corticosteroids: Systemic or inhaled corticosteroids reduce inflammation and are beneficial in conditions like acute exacerbations of asthma or COPD.
   - Antibiotics: If secondary bacterial infection is suspected, appropriate antibiotics should be administered.
4. **Decontamination:**
   - Skin Decontamination: In cases of chemical exposure, thoroughly wash the skin with soap and water to remove any residual toxins.
   - Eye Irrigation: For ocular exposure, flush the eyes with saline or water for at least 15 minutes.

LONG-TERM MANAGEMENT

1. **Monitoring and Follow-up:**
   - Regular follow-up appointments to monitor lung function and overall health.
   - Periodic imaging studies and pulmonary function tests to assess disease progression.
2. **Chronic Disease Management:**
   - Asthma: Use of long-term control medications (e.g., inhaled corticosteroids, long-acting beta-agonists) and rescue inhalers as needed.
   - COPD: Implementation of a comprehensive management plan including bronchodilators, corticosteroids, and pulmonary rehabilitation.

3. **Environmental Control:**
   - Identify and mitigate ongoing sources of exposure in the patient's environment, such as indoor air pollutants and occupational hazards.
   - Recommend measures such as air purifiers, proper ventilation, and use of PPE.
4. **Patient Education:**
   - Educate patients on the importance of avoiding triggers and adhering to treatment plans.
   - Provide resources on smoking cessation, healthy lifestyle choices, and occupational safety.

CASE EXAMPLES

1. **Case of Chronic Silica Exposure:**
   - Management: For a patient with silicosis, management includes regular monitoring of lung function, use of bronchodilators for symptom relief, and vaccinations to prevent respiratory infections.
   - Long-term Care: Pulmonary rehabilitation programs to improve respiratory function and quality of life. Referral to a specialist for advanced care if necessary.
2. **Case of Carbon Monoxide Poisoning:**
   - Acute Management: Immediate administration of 100% oxygen via a non-rebreather mask or hyperbaric oxygen therapy to displace CO from hemoglobin.
   - Follow-up: Monitoring for delayed neurological sequelae and providing supportive care.

DISCUSSION QUESTIONS

- What are the key principles in the management of respiratory toxicity, both acute and chronic? How can healthcare providers balance pharmacological interventions, supportive care, and environmental modifications to optimize patient outcomes?

- Discuss the importance of interdisciplinary collaboration in developing comprehensive treatment plans for patients affected by respiratory toxicity.

LESSON TWO: PREVENTIVE STRATEGIES IN RESPIRATORY TOXICOLOGY

Preventing respiratory toxicity is a key component of public health and clinical practice. This lesson will highlight various strategies to reduce exposure to respiratory toxins, including environmental controls, personal protective equipment (PPE), and public health initiatives.

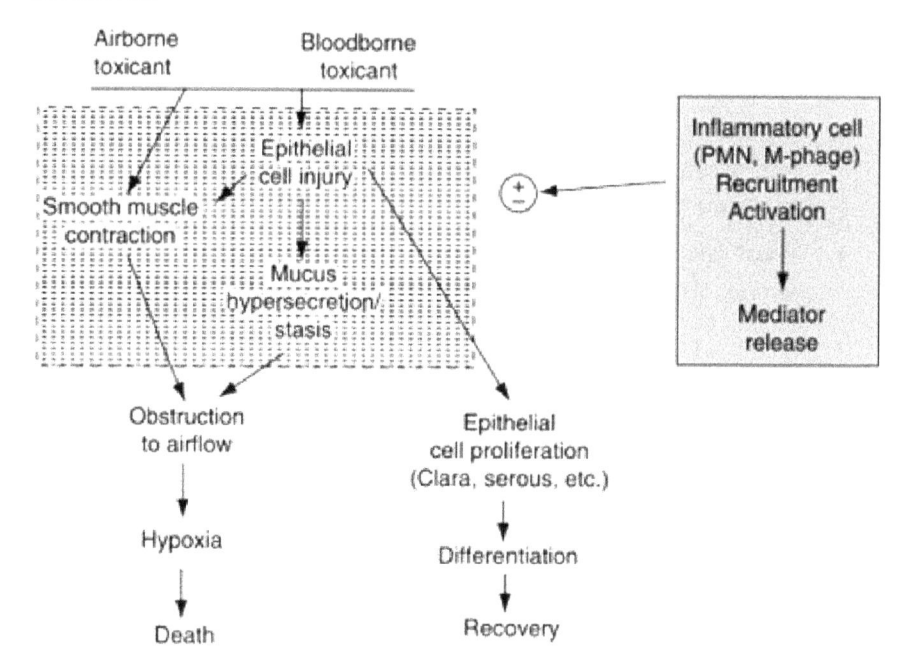

ENVIRONMENTAL CONTROLS

1. **Indoor Air Quality:**
   - Ensure proper ventilation in homes and workplaces to reduce the accumulation of indoor pollutants.
   - Use air purifiers with HEPA filters to remove particulate matter and allergens from the air.

- Avoid the use of volatile organic compounds (VOCs) by selecting low-VOC paints, cleaning agents, and building materials.

2. **Outdoor Air Quality:**
   - Support policies and regulations aimed at reducing emissions from industrial sources, vehicles, and power plants.
   - Encourage the use of alternative energy sources and green technologies to minimize air pollution.
   - Monitor air quality indices and advise patients to limit outdoor activities during high pollution days.

PERSONAL PROTECTIVE EQUIPMENT (PPE)

1. **Respirators and Masks:**
   - Use N95 respirators or higher-grade masks to protect against inhalation of hazardous particles and aerosols.
   - Ensure proper fit and training on the use of PPE to maximize effectiveness.

2. **Protective Clothing:**
   - Wear appropriate protective clothing, such as coveralls and gloves, to prevent skin exposure to toxic chemicals and dust.

PUBLIC HEALTH INITIATIVES

1. **Occupational Safety:**
   - Implement and enforce occupational health and safety regulations to protect workers from exposure to respiratory toxins.
   - Provide regular training and education on the proper use of PPE and safe work practices.

2. **Community Health Programs:**
   - Develop community-based programs to raise awareness about the sources and health effects of respiratory toxins.
   - Promote initiatives for reducing indoor and outdoor air pollution, such as tree planting and green building practices.

3. **Vaccination Programs:**

- Encourage vaccination against respiratory infections, such as influenza and pneumococcal disease, to reduce the risk of secondary complications from respiratory toxicity.

PREVENTIVE MEASURES IN SPECIFIC SETTINGS

1. **Healthcare Settings:**
   - Implement strict infection control measures to prevent the spread of respiratory pathogens.
   - Use high-efficiency particulate air (HEPA) filtration systems in areas where aerosol-generating procedures are performed.
2. **Industrial Settings:**
   - Install engineering controls, such as ventilation systems and dust suppression methods, to minimize airborne contaminants.
   - Conduct regular environmental monitoring to assess exposure levels and identify areas for improvement.
3. **Household Settings:**
   - Educate families on the safe use and storage of household chemicals to prevent accidental poisonings.
   - Promote smoking cessation programs to reduce exposure to secondhand smoke and its associated risks.

Preventive strategies are essential for reducing the incidence and impact of respiratory toxicity. By implementing environmental controls, using personal protective equipment, and supporting public health initiatives, healthcare providers can contribute to a safer and healthier environment.

DISCUSSION QUESTIONS

- What are the primary strategies for preventing respiratory toxicity in occupational and environmental settings? How can engineering controls, personal protective equipment (PPE), and workplace regulations effectively reduce exposure to respiratory toxins?

- Discuss the role of employers, regulatory agencies, and healthcare providers in promoting and enforcing preventive measures in high-risk industries.

MODULE FOUR

LESSON ONE: CASE STUDIES IN RESPIRATORY TOXICOLOGY

Case studies provide valuable insights into the practical application of theoretical knowledge in respiratory toxicology. This lesson will present several case studies that illustrate the diagnosis, management, and prevention of respiratory toxicity in real-world scenarios.

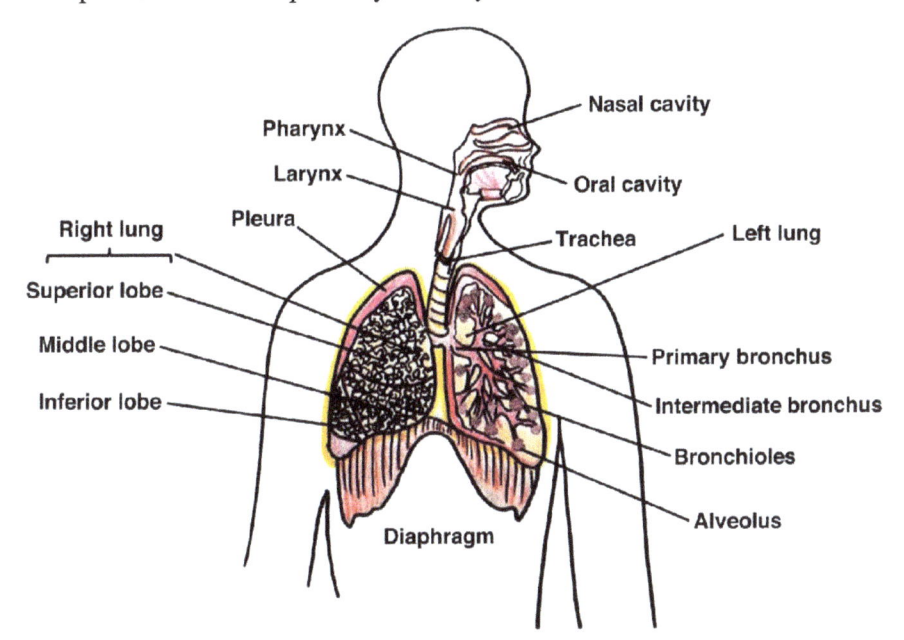

CASE STUDY 1: OCCUPATIONAL ASTHMA

Patient Profile:

A 45-year-old male factory worker presents with a two-year history of coughing, wheezing, and shortness of breath, which worsen during the workweek and improve on weekends.

Medical History:

- No prior history of asthma or other respiratory diseases.
- Works in a factory that produces cleaning chemicals.

Diagnosis:

- Spirometry shows reversible airflow obstruction.
- Peak flow monitoring demonstrates a significant decline in lung function during work hours and improvement during off-hours.

Specific IgE testing is positive for isocyanates, a known respiratory sensitizer used in the factory.

Management:

- Immediate removal from exposure to isocyanates.
- Initiation of asthma management plan, including inhaled corticosteroids and bronchodilators.
- Referral to an occupational health specialist for workplace assessment and recommendations.

Outcome:

- Significant improvement in symptoms after avoiding exposure.
- Implementation of engineering controls and use of PPE at the workplace to prevent further cases.

CASE STUDY 2: ACUTE INHALATION INJURY

Patient Profile:

A 30-year-old female presents to the emergency department with acute onset of coughing, chest pain, and difficulty breathing after a fire in her apartment.

Medical History:

- No known respiratory conditions.
- Exposed to smoke and chemical fumes during the fire.

Diagnosis:

- Physical examination reveals tachypnea, use of accessory muscles, and decreased breath sounds.
- Chest X-ray shows bilateral infiltrates suggestive of inhalation injury.
- Blood gas analysis reveals hypoxemia and respiratory acidosis.

Management:

- Immediate administration of high-flow oxygen.
- Bronchodilators and corticosteroids to reduce airway inflammation.
- Close monitoring in the intensive care unit (ICU) with potential need for mechanical ventilation.

Outcome:

- Gradual improvement in respiratory status with supportive care.
- Discharge with follow-up appointments to monitor lung function and recovery.

CASE STUDY 3: CHRONIC ASBESTOS EXPOSURE

Patient Profile:

A 65-year-old retired construction worker presents with progressive dyspnea, dry cough, and chest tightness over the past year.

Medical History:

- History of asbestos exposure during his 30-year career in construction.
- Smoked one pack per day for 40 years but quit 10 years ago.

Diagnosis:

- Physical examination reveals digital clubbing and bilateral basal crackles.

- High-resolution computed tomography (HRCT) shows pleural plaques and interstitial fibrosis.
- Pulmonary function tests indicate restrictive lung disease.

Management:

- Regular follow-up with a pulmonologist for monitoring and supportive care.
- Pulmonary rehabilitation program to improve exercise capacity and quality of life.
- Vaccination against influenza and pneumococcus to prevent respiratory infections.

Outcome:

- Stabilization of symptoms with comprehensive management.
- Ongoing monitoring for potential development of asbestos-related malignancies.

Case studies highlight the complexities and challenges of diagnosing and managing respiratory toxicity. They provide practical examples of how healthcare providers can apply theoretical knowledge to real-world situations, improving patient outcomes through timely and effective interventions.

DISCUSSION QUESTIONS

- Reflecting on the lessons learned from the case studies, what preventive strategies could have potentially mitigated the risks of respiratory toxicity for the affected individuals?
- How can healthcare providers advocate for proactive measures, such as regular monitoring, environmental assessments, and workplace safety improvements, to prevent future cases of respiratory toxicity?

MODULE FIVE

LESSON ONE: FUTURE DIRECTIONS IN RESPIRATORY TOXICOLOGY

The field of respiratory toxicology is continually evolving, driven by advances in research, technology, and our understanding of environmental health. This lesson will explore emerging trends and future directions that promise to enhance our ability to prevent, diagnose, and treat respiratory toxicities.

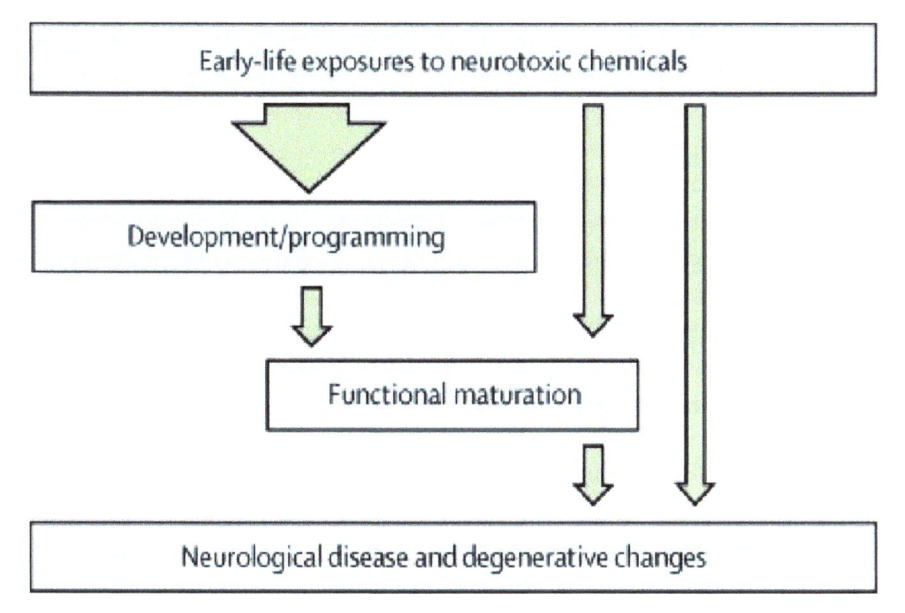

```
Early-life exposures to neurotoxic chemicals
          ↓
Development/programming
          ↓
    Functional maturation
          ↓
Neurological disease and degenerative changes
```

ADVANCES IN DIAGNOSTIC TECHNOLOGIES

Biomarkers:

- Identification of novel biomarkers for early detection of respiratory toxicity.
- Development of non-invasive tests, such as breath analysis, to detect volatile organic compounds (VOCs) indicative of exposure.

Imaging Techniques:

- Advances in high-resolution imaging modalities, such as magnetic resonance imaging (MRI) and positron emission tomography (PET), for detailed assessment of lung tissue.
- Use of artificial intelligence (AI) to analyze imaging data and improve diagnostic accuracy.

PERSONALIZED MEDICINE

Genetic Profiling:

- Understanding genetic susceptibilities to respiratory toxins through genomic studies.
- Personalized treatment plans based on individual genetic profiles, enhancing the effectiveness of interventions.

Pharmacogenomics:

- Tailoring pharmacological treatments to individual genetic variations, optimizing drug efficacy and minimizing adverse effects.
- Environmental and Public Health Initiatives

Air Quality Monitoring:

- Deployment of advanced air quality monitoring systems to provide real-time data on pollutant levels.
- Use of AI and machine learning to predict pollution patterns and inform public health interventions.

Legislation and Policy:

- Strengthening regulations to limit emissions of hazardous air pollutants from industrial and vehicular sources.
- Promoting policies that encourage the use of renewable energy and sustainable practices to reduce environmental pollution.

EMERGING THERAPEUTICS

Targeted Therapies:

- Development of novel therapies targeting specific molecular pathways involved in respiratory toxicity.
- Use of biologics and small molecules to modulate immune responses and reduce inflammation.

Regenerative Medicine:

- Advances in stem cell research and tissue engineering for the regeneration of damaged lung tissue.
- Potential use of stem cell therapies to treat chronic respiratory conditions, such as fibrosis and COPD.

PUBLIC AWARENESS AND EDUCATION

Community Engagement:

- Increased efforts to educate the public about the sources and health effects of respiratory toxins.
- Community-based programs to promote healthy behaviors and reduce exposure to environmental pollutants.

Professional Training:

- Enhanced training programs for healthcare providers on the latest developments in respiratory toxicology.
- Interdisciplinary collaboration to address complex cases of respiratory toxicity.

DISCUSSION QUESTIONS

- How can emerging technologies such as artificial intelligence (AI) and advanced imaging modalities transform the field of respiratory toxicology?
- Discuss the ethical implications of integrating AI and genomic technologies in respiratory toxicology research and clinical practice.

MODULE SIX

LESSON ONE: ETHICAL AND LEGAL CONSIDERATIONS IN RESPIRATORY TOXICOLOGY

The field of respiratory toxicology is not only driven by scientific and clinical advancements but also by ethical and legal considerations. Healthcare providers must navigate these complex aspects to ensure responsible practice and patient care.

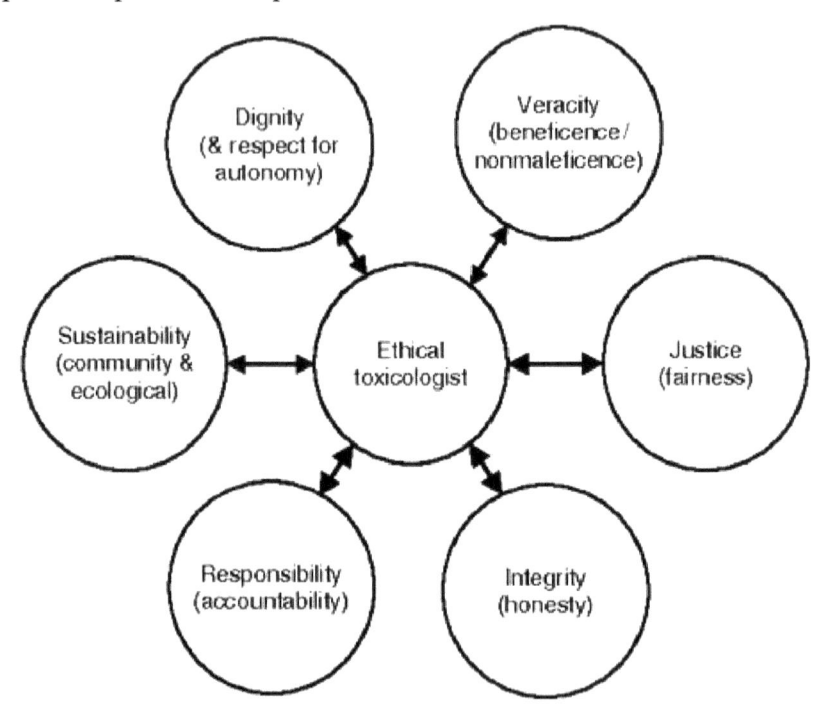

ETHICAL CONSIDERATIONS

Informed Consent:

- Patients must be fully informed about the risks, benefits, and alternatives of diagnostic tests and treatments related to respiratory toxicity.

- Ensure that patients understand their exposure history and potential long-term health effects.

Patient Autonomy:

- Respect patients' rights to make informed decisions about their care.
- Provide comprehensive education and support to help patients understand their condition and treatment options.

Confidentiality:

- Protect patient information, particularly sensitive data related to occupational and environmental exposures.
- Ensure compliance with privacy regulations, such as HIPAA in the United States.

Non-Maleficence and Beneficence:

- Strive to do no harm and act in the best interest of the patient.
- Balance the risks and benefits of interventions, considering the potential for long-term harm from certain treatments.

LEGAL CONSIDERATIONS

Regulatory Compliance:

- Adhere to local, state, and federal regulations regarding the management of hazardous substances and workplace safety.
- Stay informed about updates to laws and guidelines related to respiratory toxicology.

Reporting Obligations:

- Report cases of occupational and environmental exposure to appropriate authorities.
- Understand mandatory reporting requirements for specific toxins and conditions.

Liability and Legal Protection:

- Ensure proper documentation of patient interactions, diagnoses, and treatments.
- Be aware of legal protections available to healthcare providers and patients, such as workers' compensation and environmental laws.

Advocacy:

- Advocate for stronger regulations and policies to protect public health and prevent exposure to respiratory toxins.
- Collaborate with professional organizations and public health agencies to promote safer environments.

CASE EXAMPLES

Case of Occupational Lung Disease:

- A construction worker diagnosed with silicosis seeks compensation for medical expenses and lost wages.
- Ethical considerations include ensuring the patient is fully informed about their condition and treatment options.
- Legal considerations involve documenting the exposure history, reporting the case to occupational health authorities, and supporting the patient's claim for workers' compensation.

Case of Environmental exposure:

- A community living near an industrial plant reports increased rates of respiratory illness.
- Ethical considerations include advocating for the community's health and ensuring transparency in communicating risks.
- Legal considerations involve reporting the exposure to environmental agencies, participating in public health investigations, and supporting legal action to mitigate pollution.

Navigating ethical and legal considerations is crucial in respiratory toxicology. Healthcare providers must balance the need for patient care with regulatory compliance, patient rights, and public health advocacy. By staying informed and adhering to ethical principles, providers can deliver responsible and effective care while contributing to a safer and healthier environment.

DISCUSSION QUESTIONS

- What are the legal responsibilities of healthcare providers in reporting cases of respiratory toxicity to regulatory authorities? How can healthcare systems ensure compliance with reporting obligations while respecting patient confidentiality and privacy rights?
- Debate the role of legal protections and liability considerations in supporting healthcare providers who diagnose and treat respiratory toxicities, especially in occupational and environmental health settings.

MODULE SEVEN

LESSON ONE: INTEGRATIVE AND HOLISTIC APPROACHES TO RESPIRATORY HEALTH

In recent years, there has been growing interest in integrative and holistic approaches to respiratory health. These approaches complement conventional medical treatments and emphasize the importance of overall well-being.

NUTRITIONAL
- Herbs and supplements
- Therapeutic diets
- Prebiotics and probiotics

PSYCHOLOGICAL
- Meditation
- Hypnosis and guided imagery
- Relaxation therapies, such as breathing exercises

PHYSICAL
- Acupuncture
- Massage
- Chiropractic
- Reflexology
- Pilates

COMBINATIONS
Also known as mind-body therapies, such as:
- Music and art therapy
- Tai chi
- Mindful eating
- Dance
- Yoga
- Mindfulness-based stress reduction
- Qi gong

HOLISTIC HEALTH CONCEPTS

Mind-Body Connection:

- Recognize the interplay between mental and physical health.
- Techniques such as mindfulness, meditation, and stress reduction can positively impact respiratory conditions.

Lifestyle Modifications:

- Encourage healthy lifestyle choices, including balanced nutrition, regular exercise, and smoking cessation.
- Educate patients on the benefits of a holistic approach to respiratory health.

COMPLEMENTARY THERAPIES

Nutritional Support:

- Emphasize the role of diet in maintaining respiratory health.
- Foods rich in antioxidants, anti-inflammatory properties, and essential nutrients support lung function and reduce inflammation.

Herbal Medicine:

- Certain herbs, such as ginger, turmeric, and eucalyptus, have been shown to have beneficial effects on respiratory health.
- Integrate evidence-based herbal remedies into treatment plans, considering potential interactions with conventional medications.

Acupuncture:

- Acupuncture has been used to manage symptoms of asthma, COPD, and other respiratory conditions.
- It may help reduce inflammation, improve breathing, and enhance overall well-being.

MINDFULNESS AND STRESS REDUCTION

Breathing Exercises:

- Techniques such as diaphragmatic breathing, pursed-lip breathing, and yoga breathing can improve lung capacity and reduce stress.
- Encourage regular practice of these exercises to support respiratory health.

Mindfulness Meditation:

- Mindfulness practices help manage stress, which can exacerbate respiratory conditions.
- Regular meditation can improve mental clarity, emotional stability, and physical health.

INTEGRATIVE CARE MODELS

Patient-Centered Care:

- Develop individualized care plans that incorporate patients' preferences and values.
- Collaborate with patients to set realistic health goals and tailor interventions accordingly.

Interdisciplinary Collaboration:

- Work with a team of healthcare providers, including nutritionists, physical therapists, and mental health professionals, to provide comprehensive care.
- Ensure that all aspects of a patient's health are addressed, promoting holistic well-being.

CASE EXAMPLES

Case of Chronic Asthma:

- A patient with poorly controlled asthma incorporates dietary changes, regular yoga practice, and mindfulness meditation into their routine.

- Over time, they experience improved symptom control, reduced reliance on rescue inhalers, and enhanced quality of life.

Case of COPD:

- A COPD patient participates in a pulmonary rehabilitation program that includes breathing exercises, nutritional counseling, and acupuncture.
- The integrative approach leads to improved lung function, reduced breathlessness, and better overall health.

Integrative and holistic approaches offer valuable tools for enhancing respiratory health. By incorporating complementary therapies, lifestyle modifications, and mind-body practices, healthcare providers can support patients in achieving optimal well-being. Embracing a holistic perspective allows for comprehensive care that addresses the physical, mental, and emotional aspects of respiratory health.

DISCUSSION QUESTIONS

- How can healthcare providers tailor integrative care plans to meet the individual needs and preferences of patients with respiratory conditions? What role do patient education and empowerment play in promoting adherence to holistic treatment approaches?
- Debate the ethical considerations in recommending and practicing integrative therapies alongside evidence-based treatments in respiratory health, ensuring patient safety and informed decision-making.

CONCLUSION

Respiratory toxicology stands at a critical juncture, balancing the complexities of understanding, diagnosing, and managing the myriad factors that impact respiratory health. This comprehensive exploration has underscored the vital need for a multidisciplinary approach that combines advances in medical research, technology, ethical considerations, and patient-centered care to effectively address the challenges posed by respiratory toxins.

Throughout the lessons, we have journeyed from the fundamental principles of respiratory toxicology to the latest advancements in diagnostics, treatment strategies, and preventive measures. The importance of understanding the pathophysiology of respiratory toxicity has been highlighted, revealing how toxins can disrupt cellular processes and lead to severe health outcomes. We have also delved into the diagnostic landscape, exploring how advancements in biomarkers, imaging, and genetic profiling are enhancing our ability to detect and manage respiratory toxicity early and accurately.

The journey through respiratory toxicology has reinforced the critical need for ongoing research, education, and collaboration. By embracing a holistic and forward-thinking approach, we can enhance our understanding, improve diagnosis, and develop more effective treatments, ultimately ensuring better respiratory health for individuals and communities worldwide. This dynamic field continues to evolve, and it is our collective responsibility to remain vigilant, informed, and proactive in our efforts to combat the threats posed by respiratory toxins

REFERENCES

Antonini, J. M. (2021). *Respiratory Toxicology of Occupational and Environmental Agents. CRC Press.*

Balmes, J. R., & Abraham, J. L. (Eds.). (2020). *Occupational and Environmental Lung Diseases: Diseases from Work, Home, Outdoor and Other Exposures. Springer.*

Burchiel, S. W., & Carakostas, M. C. (Eds.). (2016). *Comprehensive Toxicology. Elsevier.*

Calverley, P. M., & Wedzicha, J. A. (Eds.). (2016). *Respiratory Medicine: Clinical Cases Uncovered. John Wiley & Sons.*

Costa, D. L., & Barry, B. E. (Eds.). (2017). *Toxicology of the Nose and Upper Airways. CRC Press.*

Harkema, J. R., & Plopper, C. G. (Eds.). (2014). *Comparative Biology of the Normal Lung. Academic Press.*

Nriagu, J. O. (Ed.). (2018). *Encyclopedia of Environmental Health. Elsevier.*

Riediker, M., & Zinsstag, J. (Eds.). (2020). *Occupational and Environmental Health: Recognizing and Preventing Disease and Injury. Oxford University Press.*

Milton Keynes UK
Ingram Content Group UK Ltd.
UKHW050309140724
445568UK00009B/53